BENBROOK PUBLIC LIBRARY

3 4267 00013 5710

D1508920

BENBROOK PUBLIC LIBRARY

ALSO BY BROOKS HAXTON

Poetry

The Sun at Night
Traveling Company
Dead Reckoning
Dominion
The Lay of Eleanor and Irene

Translations

Fragments: The Collected Wisdom of Heraclitus
Dances for Flute and Thunder: Praises, Prayers, and Insults

NAKEDNESS, DEATH, AND THE NUMBER ZERO ❧

NAKEDNESS, DEATH, AND THE NUMBER ZERO

Poems by
Brooks Haxton

Alfred A. Knopf
New York
2001

THIS IS A BORZOI BOOK PUBLISHED BY ALFRED A. KNOPF

Copyright © 2001 by Brooks Haxton
All rights reserved under International and Pan-American Copyright
Conventions. Published in the United States by Alfred A. Knopf, a division
of Random House, Inc., New York, and simultaneously in Canada by Ran-
dom House of Canada Limited, Toronto. Distributed by Random House,
Inc., New York.

www.randomhouse.com/knopf/poetry
Knopf, Borzoi Books, and the colophon are registered
trademarks of Random House, Inc.

Grateful acknowledgment is made to the following publications, where
some of these poems originally appeared:
The Atlantic Monthly: "Molybdenum" and "Sanskrit at First Snowfall";
Barrow Street: "Memorizing Lycidas Under the Warhol at the Walker";
New England Review: "Author's Bio"; *The New Republic:* "Catalpa"; *The
New Yorker:* "Clearing After Dark," "Salesmanship, with Half a Dram of
Tears"; *Ohio Review:* "I Swore My Love on the Appointed Day"; *The
Ontario Review:* "Teenage Ikon"; *The Paris Review:* "It Comes to Me:
Concision!"; *Partisan Review:* "November Seasonal" and "Seasonal";
Triquarterly: "Tweeg."

Library of Congress Cataloging-in-Publication Data
Haxton, Brooks.
Nakedness, death, and the number zero : poems / by Brooks Haxton.
p.   cm.
ISBN 0-375-41248-4 (hardcover) — ISBN 0-375-70956-8 (pbk.)
I. Title.
PS3558.A825 N34 2001
811'.54—dc21   2001033892

Manufactured in the United States of America
First Edition

Acknowledgments
Thanks to my friends, especially to those who helped me see these poems
through revision: Joe-Anne McLaughlin Carruth, Roger Fanning, Pamela
Greenberg, Mary Karr, Susan Kolodny, and Andy Robbins. Deborah Garri-
son at Knopf has helped to make this book far better than it would have
been without her guiding intelligence. As always, thanks to my wife and
family, without whom this work would have been unimaginable.

For Isaac, Miriam, and Lillie

Contents

AS FAR
AS I COULD TELL

. . . the frog wept with all his skin,
so happy, so helpless: not dead, not dead.

—Roger Fanning

As Far As I Could Tell

After they pulled my wisdom tooth both eyeballs
ached into their moorings. Something with spurs
had lodged behind my eardrum. Dawn came, vague
with codeine and the sound of rain, sheets drenched.
I had to be reminded what this meant.
Francie nudged me, "Brooks, my water broke."

In the delivery room that afternoon
wrack of childbirth put toothache to shame.
No screams, but Francie sang with it,
a riven octave higher than her speaking voice.
Her blood splashed onto the doctors' shoes.

Someone we had never met held up our daughter
Miriam by the shanks, terrifyingly pale blue
and cheesy in her varnish, with her arms hung down.

The doctors' hands pushed into the dough of Francie's belly
where it had been taut, and shifted down Twin B,
whose head in a loop of cord pinched off the bloodflow
into her brain. Francie, forceps huge,
tearing between her legs, still sang. She pushed,
and beads of sweat stood quivering in her face.

Lillie came out smaller, bluer, wearier.
The doctors handed Miriam to me
to show her mother, while they worked on Lillie
who had made no sound. Francie, not yet stitched,

lay calm, blood trickling into a large pool
on the floor. I held up Miriam, and felt

my toothache throb, the surge inside my chest,
fear building. Codeine made no difference.
Francie shivered. It was raining, nightfall.
I was kissing her, with Miriam
between us in my arms. And Lillie cried.

Molybdenum

(mŏ lĭb' dĕ nŭm; mŏ lĭb dē' nŭm; mə lib' də nəm)

The year before Chernobyl I spent evenings
abstracting translations of reports
by engineers on Soviet nuclear power plants.
Many times I typed the word *molybdenum*,
uncertain how it might be said.

Three dollars an item, eight items an hour,
faking the Authoritative Version,
I felt queasy, that a phrase deleted
might make dangerous misinformation
of the nonsense in my head.

This was the year of our first baby, when I worked
four jobs, and wrote before dawn every day
devotions on the hours and pastiches
of Lao Tzu, the sense of the originals
as vague to me as anything in the reports.

That next year, in a magazine, I saw
the radiation babies, stillborn, and in pain,
and yellowish eruptions on the forearm
of a young man poisoned cleaning up.
He died, the caption said, in seven months.

And still, I want to make my part make sense,
the way men stay at work to keep their jobs:
one wrings plutonium into a bucket
with his bare hands; and another
writes about it for no one to read.

Catalpa

Nobody saw him, leaning from his wheelchair into the pain
  just as his one-time partner's hip swung into reach.
He drew, and quickly slipping barrel first into his mouth
    showed everybody in the stationhouse
      exactly how the thing is done.

The money from his death came late, too late
      to help his daughter, thrown
    too many years before head first, they said
      she threw herself, who knows
how stoned she was, head first, four stories down
    into the bare yard of her tenement.

  And now, my friend, his other daughter,
  tried all weekend, failed again, and tried
      to reach her brother for the holiday.
He lived alone, inheritance, the remnant, sunk by now
      into a farmhouse where the phone rang,
and he drank. His ex-wife told my friend:
    he drank, and took however long it took
      that weekend with his gun
  to demonstrate again their father's point.

  And now my friend, alive, a thousand miles away,
    saw sunlight through the bare catalpa,
        ghost pods swinging
under the shadows of the branches on the closet door,

and she was glad to see them, although people say,
about catalpa pods this time of year,
gone brown and crooked, dangling, swinging,
scattered, broken by the wind, over the frozen grass,
that they are ugly. And it's true. They are.

Nakedness, Death, and the Number Zero

Archimedes, having failed to calculate the volume
of King Hieron's golden wreath, quit work, emptied
his mind, and eased himself into a brimful bath.
Let the custodian fret how much I spill, he thought,
and more sloshed out the more of him went under, volume
spilled precisely that of the parts of him submerged.
Eureka! Naked, into the sunlit streets of Syracuse,
he skipped forth, modestly cupping his genital
in one hand, shouting: *Eureka! I have found!*—it,
displacement volumetrics, being to Archimedes
understood. But onlookers could only cluck:
How sad, in middle age, to find one's genital,
and lose one's mind. His mind kept clicking, though,
until a soldier hacked his neck with that new
Spanish sword, the gladius. But he was old by then.
The Romans, having laid siege to the city for two years,
now sacked it, and killed thousands. Zero, as a numeral
which indicates the difference between volumes in a bath
before and after one's submersion, is a concept
Archimedes in the meantime never knew. He died
two centuries before the absence of a year between
year minus one and year plus one. An Indian accountant,
I have read, first marked the empty place *sunya,*
and Arab traders, calling this mark *sifr,* brought it
West, where everybody took to ciphering in no time.
Zero flourished in the Dark Age and the Renaissance.
The numeral took root wherever reckonings were made.
Businessmen used zeroes without minding what they meant.

Soon after the Enlightenment, among Romantics, zero
as an idea dawned on Europe. Doctrine formed. Division
into zero, and by zero, zero parts of zero, overflowed
into a greater nonexistence where the empty set
lay empty of infinities and finitudes and of itself.

Now and Again

1. Dry Spell, 2 A.M.

The dusty cricket Meleager heard,
   awake like this, asking himself
   where Heliodora was with whom,

   he promised, next day
he would give a cooling drink,

   if only the cricket song
     could help him sleep.

   Now, dust of Meleager
indistinct from Heliodora's
   dust, the cricket sings.

2. Noon

   Night shrank
  into the yew hedge
spattered with white paint.

3. Beside the Pond

   Three blackbirds sprang
from the lowest long branch,
  and an old carp, lifting
   into air a face the age
    of my face, plucked

a mulberry. He too had seen it
   dabbled under the birds'
      weight into the image
   of heaven where they flew.

4. *Tick*

   Inside the clock
a metal flange scraped
   over the crest of one
   tooth in the gearwheel
and thwacked into the next.

5. *Luck*

   The graveyard in the window
filled with snow. A boy inside
      at midnight asked a girl
if he could hold her. Nodding
      yes, who knows? she stepped
into the space between his arms.

Memorizing "Lycidas" Under the Warhol at the Walker

Though no one I had met believed it genuine, it gave me goosebumps.
I was learning the flower passage, and my shift was ending,
when the next guard caught me with my xerox reading on the job,
aloud, how "daffadillies fill their cups with tears." I saw:
he heard me. Pausing, pointing at me, he said, "Wait!
'To strew the laureate hearse where Lycid lies.' " I didn't
know the man, but thought his name was Craig, or Greg.
Deliberate inflection counterpoised against the meter,
closing his eyes, he said: "Weep no more, woeful Shepherds,
weep no more, For Lycidas your sorrow is not dead," *dead*
emphasized with feinted resolution—then, on the upbeat:
"*Sunk* though he be beneath the wat'ry floor," and with a leap
in pitch: "*So* sinks the day-star in the Ocean bed, And yet
anon repairs his drooping head"—I can remember still
the way he held that high note in the second syllable: "re*pairs*
his drooping head, And tricks his beams, and with new-spangled Ore,
Flames in the forehead of the morning sky." He stepped down
beat by beat in pitch, and stopped, and looked for me to speak.
"Do you write poems?" "No," he smiled apologetically, "do you?"

Salesmanship, with Half a Dram of Tears

Gripping the lectern, rocking it, searching
the faces for the souls, for signs of heartfelt
mindfulness at work, I thought, as I recited
words I wrote in tears: instead of tears,
if I had understood my father's business,
I could be selling men's clothes. I could be
kneeling, complimenting someone at the bay
of mirrors, mumblingly, with pinpoints pressed
between my lips. That was the life I held
in scorn while young, because I thought to live
without distraction, using words. Yet, looking
now into the room of strangers' eyes, I wanted
them to feel what I said touch, as palpably
as when a man in double worsted felt
the cuff drop to his wrist. There was a rush
in the applause of gratitude and mercy:
they could go. A teenager, embarrassed
for himself and me, lefthandedly
squeezed my fingers, and said thanks.

Consort

When the old moon saw
her brother earth bathed
in blue-green flame, her gone
face smoldered back, "Now,
only friend, my darkness
opens me again toward you."
He turned to her, and she to him.
They turned. And turned away.
Cloudswirls. Stars flared out.
They never touched, nor could they
be more conjugal than this.

Song of the Rose

Her memory of the rose
may yet grow less from little,
for all her husband knows,

though to his mind what grows
more troubling, like a riddle
in his memory, is the rose

bruised under the blows
he dealt her. No acquittal,
no tenderness he knows

can mend, no plea transpose,
or make the least less brittle,
her memory of the rose.

Blooms full-blown may close,
and love turn noncommittal.
This, by now, he knows.

Since, when she left, they chose
to let the lawyers settle,
her memory of the rose
is hers: that's all he knows.

Professor of History

Frank Randall, Ph.D.,
in Haiti for his holiday
in a local plane at night
over the attractive sea
with Ariel his teenage girl,
off course, out of gas, fell
into the blue gone black
and solid where they struck.
Their pilot with an open skull
took the plane below,
the *clairin* and his blood
unraveling in the dark.
Four of the five swam free,
one with a bad gash in her brow,
wearying, confused.
Another thought to help
the injured woman wait.
Maybe the ship they saw
had radioed for rescue.
Frank and Ari made
for the little lights on shore.
They swam that night all night,
and slowly that next day
by nightfall neared tall palms
when a storm from the island
came carrying them out,
apart, on separate waves,
their throats too dry to shout.
This was the second night

Frank would stay alive
to save his Ari if he could.
By dawn, the markers gone
between Frank's dreaming
and this world, he looked
through a delicate spiraling
structure into the upward blue
where waiters floating offered him
exotic drink and food.
Faces dark above him
spoke a cryptic tongue.
He felt his legs, his body,
lift, and wobble somewhere
low, inside a narrow boat.
Whether the pirogues and the men
in ragged clothes had come
from the island or from his dream,
he did not ask, or care.
He went with them, away.
Meeting his Ari then
on shore, oblivion
stewing in his brain,
he saw her see him, saved,
neither of them pleased,
she no more than he,
(there was excitement somewhere),
they no more than the pilot
settling his plane
in the dark on the floor,

or the lady who hit her head
and did not wish to swim,
or the other who chose to stay
with someone she had met that day,
to wait with her for help.
What came instead we saw
behind Frank's face at school.
He caught me watching it in his eyes
when I said, "Good to see you, Frank."
I was listening for it in his voice
when he said, "Good to be seen."

First Thing

Where nothing was, a flower
the size of a human face:
five crimson petals,
gaps between them
forming a star
of five green eyes of flame,
the sepals backlit.
Later, beaten limp by rain,
snapped off, and brought inside,
the flower in its vase revived,
with petals fully spread,
which even on the branch alive
would have to crumple shut
the second day.

TEENAGE IKON ❧

When he took me drinking in the woods,
he showed me tracks of animals
and shapes of nests. He knew
about convolvulus, psilocybes,
and jimson weed, enough, at least,
to pick what brought on visions.

After the rain quit, overflowing
mud-blond current from the river settled
in the backwaters into a deep tea green
as clear as we would ever see it.
We could spend all day adrift,
the rowboat filled with willow shade,
where twenty thousand straight treetrunks
in all directions stood neck-deep
or deeper in the flood. Black
flutterings with gurgled notes
of redwings everywhere.
Calm water. Pale green
overcast of willow branches.

Who we were at home, how small
we felt beside our older brothers,
how we worried what girls made of us
at school, such eggheads, such unkempt,
unruly boys: who cared?—the coot,
the summer tanager, the wood duck?

Not a soul, not here. So
here we came, to smoke weed
and to fish, to swim,
smoke cigarettes and drink,
talk easy talk, or not talk
sometimes, sometimes not for hours.

Sixteen, up and out of sight
across the water before daybreak,
we stayed out past dusk,
when we would build a fire,
and cook the channel cat or bass
we caught, or stole from who-knows-whose
trot line, or whose gill net. Or fillets
of rattler, if he shot one with his pistol—
these well-charred and washed down
with white lightning strong enough
it ate the bottom off a paper cup
unless we used two thick.

No moon. Calm. Insect roar dissolved
in starlight. Whippoorwill, owl, bullfrog,
treefrog. Nearby, snap and hiss
of burning wood, and slide and slap
of water on the sandbar, his voice
singing "Don't Think Twice,"
and mine reciting:

I have heard the mermaids singing, each to each.
I do not think that they will sing to me.

We were liars, thieves,
but when he stole my fishing gear,
and when he lied about time spent with her,
the one I said I loved, I felt sparks
flick inside my palm, making my hand a fist.

Later, by the river after midnight,
when I spread a blanket on the sandbar
for the girl he told me he would marry,
hardshell Baptist's daughter that she was,
she shifted toward me on one side,
and streaks among the stars, the Perseids,
flared two or three at once,
as incandescent as heat lightnings
on the mile-wide tremor of the Mississippi.

That next week he came for me
with magic mushrooms, and euphoria flowed
through my hands out of the slick sides
of a bluegill, vision of obsidian
and apricot, moss green and grizzle—
ikon of the holy flesh, a god
from which I chopped the head. I plunged
my forefinger into the belly, burst
the airsack, hooked, and pulled, and all
the different colored organs popped loose,

floating through the dark green water
downward in a slow galactic swirl.

It was August, late, the river fallen,
shady low edge of the willow woods
far up the bank, the once-dark mud
grown thick by now with dust and weeds
where we had pulled the boat ashore,
not talking, cleaned, and cooked,
and eaten what we caught, the afternoon sun
drifting toward night into the willows.

Slowly, as the shade swept down the bank,
he took the pistol from the tackle box,
and turned it over in his hands,
a twenty-two revolver. In a daze
I watched while he unlatched
the cylinder, and swung it free
to dump the cartridges in one palm.

"I packed these," he said,
"made the noses pointed,
greased them too—for penetration."

One, he tossed across the fire for me to see.
Another, having touched it to his tonguetip,
he slipped into the cylinder, which he spun shut.
"Where she stops nobody knows: right?"

I had seen him practice this.
He could spin a cartridge once,
or twice, or three times round
to stop exactly under the hammer. Now,
he was giving me a cold smile. "These
I packed with a double charge."

He sighted on the fire, and then my face,
and cocked the hammer with his thumb.
"What do you think: more muzzle velocity,
or does the whole thing blow up in my hand?"

"Please. You don't want to shoot me."

"No? All right then, shoot yourself."
He sailed the pistol, cocked,
straight through the fire into my lap.

Catching it with both hands,
I could hear in slo-mo
of adrenaline and psilocybin
a minute slip of the hammer
free, before it slammed
into the knuckle of my little finger,
muzzle snug against my gut.

Shade covered him by now.
But standing from the fire
he was immersed again,

his upper torso and his face,
in warm hallucinated sunlight.

"I should drag your ass into the goddamn fire."

"I'm sorry." I was looking down,
putting the pistol in the tackle box,
and under the glow of mushrooms, feeling
pain throb in my little finger.
When I stood, I walked down past him
toward the boat, and when I turned around
to look, the sun over his shoulder made him
a vague human shape of darkness.

He'd be fifty, if he's still alive.
I saw him twenty years ago in a fern bar,
just before I moved away. On a night
that warm, he must have worn long sleeves
to hide the tracks, but he looked good.

I was close enough, I overheard him
tell three half-drunk college girls
what a trip it was in August like this,
in a heat wave, when you dive for salvage
in the pitch black under the Mississippi.
Alligator gar, some twelve feet long,
are down there, you can't see them,
cruising for their dinner,
and a predator like that survives

two hundred million years
because, come dinner, nothing stops him.
But they're not a problem, really.
They're just there. The problem is more
in your head. You're tired. You're cold.
A few yards up, it's ninety-nine degrees,
and here you are exhausted, shivering,
a few yards under the midday glare
in total darkness, with no inkling of direction.
And the current's no help either. It keeps
swirling, changing. That's what gets you
tired, and turned around, and scared,
and then whichever way you swim,
the panic just gets worse.

"That's too weird," one girl interrupted him,
and they were all three spooked.

He shrugged, and thought out loud
maybe he'd win some money playing darts.
He was standing, turning, when our eyes
met that last time, his shifting quickly
to my partner. We could pass
in straight bars, even redneck bars,
but he was reading us, of course,
and something, I could feel it
in his cold smile, clicked.

I SWORE MY
LOVE ON THE
APPOINTED DAY ❧

Here you are my best man, Harris,
in the snapshot Francie framed and hung
over the crapper, her bouquet
held up behind your head
in smiling Harpo-Marxist salutation.

         *

Children strewed the lawn that day with petals
of expensive flowers. Fresh from their divorce
my parents, and my brother newly married, soon
to be divorced, bearing a standard for the huppah,

smiled. The father of the bride, though disapproving,
smiled. Advisedly, I swore my love. I swore it
by the War God of dead goatfarmers. I swore,
you heard me, and I crushed the empty glass.

         *

And now my babies downstairs, my twin girls,
are getting their morning bath, a ceremony
that makes them, if this could be, more beautiful
for how in turn they lie back smiling at Francie,
with all but their faces under the lukewarm water.

         *

Last night Isaac said, "You're scaring me.
Please. Stop." After he went to bed,
we started again. His mother spit
into my face, while I talked babytalk
to mock her, and the babies watched.

Later, jolted from a dream, Isaac,
screaming, ran to his mother's bed:
"I want to die. I'd rather kill myself
than think about it, that I have to die."
He woke the babies. Francie scolded him,

and sent him back to sleep. His dad—
who helped him learn to speak, to feel
this way at eight—slept on a pallet
in the white noise of the attic fan.

&

In my favorite *Judgment* at the Met
damned souls stream out of the giant bones
of a spreadeagle skeleton suspended underground
on the abyss, like a white dangling spider.
Demons below that in a heap of bodies
worry with sharp claws and teeth
whoever maddening writhes near them.

Over the pit, in rapture, corpses
rise from underground and underwater

into the luckier venue in the sky.
One in a velvet robe with lush fur trim
looks singularly welcome, kneeling on the cloud
among glad angels at the left of Jesus:

this soul, I would guess, made van Eyck
many florins happier to see him
in that tier of heaven. Whom shall *I* pay, Harris,
barkeep, psychoanalyst, or gourmet grocer,
mortgage banker, ticket agent—oh,

and what about my student animatedly,
in conversation, laying one hand
just above my knee, her fingertips
along the inside seam, the muscles
in her neck like sculpture, eyes blue,
dilating: it's not my middle age
the way I pictured it
in sixty-eight, the year we met,
but here it is with an irrefutable logic.

❧

You, while I've been writing, with Cheyenne
to celebrate your anniversary have hiked
along the Great Divide and caught
sweet trout for supper, pitched camp,
and looked up at night from high among the Rockies
into the gearbox of the cosmos, then, again,

you tell me, after daylong bickering,
into each other's eyes.

༁

With my luck—Lillie the joker,
weighing at her birth not five pounds,
perfect! and at six months, limp
with a fever close to killing her
so that she could not form a smile
for weeks, now, laughing again—
Mama, her forehead at the touch
of the windshield torn back
from the skull, whole body bruised,
and stitched and stapled, now,
with my luck, mended—none
of us past mending—even Francie
taking me back to bed this afternoon,
my life's work at my desk
with its imaginary pain and pleasure still
for thirty years returning almost
every day—my luck: such luck
foolhardiness itself would not expect.
I disapprove of saying, with such
luck, that I want anything. I swore
my love on the appointed day by Him
whose vengeance and whose mercy is
that He does not exist. I do.

WHAT IF THE OLD LOVE SHOULD RETURN ☙

Quid si priscia redit Venus?

—Horace

The Ghosts of Voices Bounced off Satellites
and Swarmed Toward Earth

One with the tiniest whistle of a lisp
returned out of the solar wind
to shiver the little bones inside my ear.
Your voice, forgotten
years ago, came back

as clear as nightfall
in each other's arms:
a nighthawk *woof!* veered up
and did not burst into the star
that wobbled over the quarry pond.

What fused inside that star did burst.
And after years you called from nowhere.
You! From Vega starlight,
traveling since the time of our first touch,
struck into me and stopped.

I Told My Wife

I've always wished,
as all men wish,
to do her wrong.
And if I did,
I'd say I never did.

I never did.
For twenty years
I never kissed but one
of all those mouths
so achingly so near.

Whatever lies
I tell, I swear,
I'm faithful always
to the ring of truth.

Nightjar

That first time we made love, nighthawks
dove from out of sight among the stars
and just before they struck the earth
swerved up—the *woof* in their wingfeathers
like Ben Webster's fluttering way down on the sax.

Nightjar is their family name,
because their calling jars the night;
the whip-poor-will and chuck-will's-widow
make me think of you, that whistle far off
in your lisp, calling from nowhere.

And the poor-will (which I've never seen nor heard)
repeats his double-note out West near you.
My field guide says he's boring. When you hear

his repetitious cry and whistle your note back,
I want to say, I'll be there with you, but I won't.

I Thought of Ovid Whining in His Exile, When You Said You
Missed Me Now, Three Decades Since You Broke My Heart

Ovid told a few young wives, his readers, how
they might most pleasurably cheat their husbands,
and they did. The Son of God, Augustus, then
sent Ovid east. Only a fool would think
those last poems from the Black Sea transcend exile,

every word sent back to Rome, where Ovid dared not
ask that he be sent: a few miles nearer might be
less like death, he said. In Pontus, he was dying,
while his pleas, which failed to get him home, squeaked
like wingbones in their sockets, carrying him

neither here nor there. But outside Time, they say,
the throats of whip-poor-wills and human beings
vibrate in the Cosmic Harp. And you and I,
just now, where were we, when a voice
without a body whispered, Are you with me?

Midnight, Showering in the Boys' Dorm,
After We Had Laughed and Shushed

You stepped behind me, soaping my belly,
stroking me with your soapy hands,

wet breasts sliding under my wingbones,
and I soared. I wish that flight
could come back in these words.
I felt your haunch
glide under my palm. Slip.
Slowly. You, when I turned
toward you, smiled.
And turned away.

Spin

Roast duckling braised in port,
boiled new potatoes in their skins,
asparagus, blanched warm
with garlic butter, and Bordeaux:

but for the nine states,
and the years between us,
I would cook you such a meal . . .

although you may be
vegetarian, read prose,
and drink no stronger drink
than rose hip tea.

It's just as well.
A spinning mind is all I have
to give you. Here.

Your Favorite Job, You Told Me, Was Tree Surgeon
for the City of Chicago

I can see you in your helmet climb
the sycamore, the namesake here
of the Egyptian fig which was the Tree
of Heaven. Overhead, you lean
again from emptiness not quite
within my reach, gear gleaming.
Under the low blue vault

inside the tomb of Ramses
once, I saw the golden stars
in Nut's belly, and her breast,
and armpit. Geb, the Earth,
lay on his back, his manhood
upright towards her, longer
than the long bone in his leg.

The Sungod Re, made jealous
by their fucking,
had set Emptiness
between them—Stargoddess
arched naked over Earth
on fingertip and toe,
just out of reach.

Emptiness, clothed
as a young man of high birth,
had kneeled on him to lift her
as if Heaven might be
borne away forever
without effort. Seed leaves
sprouted through Geb's ribcage.

Emptiness, the story goes,
enthralls the world,
until diseased,
and hated by his followers,
he abdicates. Then, Geb,
the Earth, in proper clothing,
becomes Good King,

Patron, I read somewhere,
of the Scribe,
whom he transforms in pain
to entertain the gods.

Falling Leaves Made Tinctures in the Early Snow

Heavy packing snapped limbs from the dogwood
and uprooted one old honeysuckle by the back door.
In the blacked-out houses, candlelight. Then,
wash of lightnings without thunder, blue,
then green, and slow. The girls were scared:
they're two. We cuddled on the couch, and Isaac

pointed out their mother's candle upstairs,
wobbling the shadows in the entrance hall.
I had in mind a spring snow poem from China.
Su Tung P'o, younger than I, saw snowfall
on pear blossoms. This was a thousand years ago.
He wondered, in his widowerhood, in exile,
how many springs a man might see before he died.

The Pilgrimage of Young Orpheus

You said goodbye, fat good
in that, a dry kiss, your lips
fresh from his. Blubbering,
I trudged on crusted snow
away. My plane tipped queasily
over the North Atlantic. Months:
a room I rented by the week,
a job I quit. I hitched off
into the spring rain, guided
by strangers south and east.
And of the writ of Orphic Hymns
burned for a cookfire
in the sacred library
at Pergamum, I could not stir
one syllable in the dust.

Aubade of the Word Made Flesh

Words, the learned say,
may sing themselves apart from us.

Don't stop, you said.
And I sang you

what I could
over the Ozarks

down the Rockies, west,
where dawn with a glance

from the river
rippled the ceiling

over you in bed.
Hands stir

under the white sheet
of this page,

behind the blue
profusion, stars.

In Rhetoric, Adynaton Declares the Matter Inexpressible

What I wanted to tell you was
by New Year's 1996 the snowfall,
nine feet, was a record: now,
it's raining, melting, flooding,
high wind. Look! If I could tell you
how I feel, maybe I wouldn't have to search
between the stitches in the window ice
and ransack disused languages for scraps
of God. Dead limbs snapped from the catalpa
read against this morning's pockmarked snow
like scribblings in Sumerian, or like this poem,
when what I feel is no more words
than it is math or bird cries.

In My Dream, After I Made You Cry

The touch of a wingstroke on the pond
shattered the constellations east.

You Said You Liked It When You Heard the Trains

    A minor chord bends in the dark
between the left hand of Chopin and that most hidden,
      subtlest of all flesh inside your ear.
        Then, Jelly Roll comes
barrelhousing into the full Sonora moonlight.
      Where, by what light, what sounds move you,

in this poem, only my words can say. Dante said
   that Beatrice booked him passage living
      through the hoops of Hell,
    below the lake of spiritual ice,
      beyond the swiftest heavens
        and the white rose
    penetrated everywhere with light,
until he *saw* Love in the threefold fire of being.
Beatrice, for her part, had never met the man.
   She, long since, married someone else, and died.
     But that was only in the world, in time.
       So, I was thinking,
   we could maybe swing a trip like theirs. But now
     it's late. Along the river
    under the desert stars a little wind
carries the jolt of couplings from a westbound freight.

TWEEG ॐ

tweeg [Lenape *tuechque, twi'kw.*] The hellbender.
hellbender A large aquatic salamander . . .
salamander A lizardlike animal once popularly sup-
posed to be able to live in fire; hence a mythical and not
clearly defined animal having the power to endure fire
without harm.

—*Webster's New International Dictionary,*
Second Edition

Fire A symbol of transformation and regeneration . . .
an image of energy which may be found at the level of
animal passion as well as on the plane of spiritual
strength. . . . It implies the desire to annihilate time and
to bring all things to their end.

—Cirlot's *Dictionary of Symbols*

Placed . . . in alcohol for a day . . . hellbenders displayed
their hardiness by not only emerging alive but moving
about with unexpected activity.

—De Sola's *American Wild Life*

After his third wife left him, Dr. Yearner
set up the dental island in his garage,
which cost him business, but he wanted privacy
at work. I liked to visit him when I was small

and feed the fish. It was a huge tank with such
tiny fish, the hellbender I gave him struck me,
at thirteen, as the very creature of his dreams,
though he had never seen one. It's for you,

our largest native salamander, I said, dropping it in.
He stood back, blinking, while it ate the fairy basslet.
In a few days all the fish were gone. The old man
I saw catch it, seining, told me Tweeg was the name

the Indians had given it. Tweeg, an arm long,
with minute black eyes set into a paleozoic skull,
alert with mindlessness. The skin fit loosely
in deep folds, greenish brown with warts and slime.

The fingers had no claws, but he was strong enough to catch
and eat a crawdad. Snails too, worms and tadpoles,
anything alive that came to hand, he ate, and he grew fat.
My pubic hair was coming in, and soon my wisdom teeth

plowed into my molars sideways, skewing
my lowers in the front like headstones
in the Johnson grass beside the rendering plant.
Dr. Yearner, having pulled a few in back,

saw chips in the enamel on my dog teeth.
He thought I was snapping in my sleep.
I didn't know. I wouldn't, would I?
Dr. Yearner had a kind smile. He said,

No. At any rate, gold tips would do the job.
They looked good too. I trusted him, the Doctor,
even when he got the shakes. My smile
at seventeen, I would have said, looked elegant.

Soigné was the word the Doctor used.
But being drunk, he left some rot in one,
that festered up the nerve, and up, for years,
until it ate a dime-sized hole out through my upper jaw.

I was working then part-time, and living at home.
My parents spoke through me. "Ask your mother
to pass the turnip greens, Carl." "Tell
your father he dropped oyster on his lapel."

After they went up to bed some nights
I heard them struggling quietly in there,
as if to kill whatever-it-was alive
they kept between them. Neverminding that,

at thirty-five, I fell in love with Gwen,
my teenage cousin. Mother had always said Gwen's flesh
was porcelain. Father said not, not in its warmth.
Her eyes also, and her intelligence, were warm

and luculent. When she began to speak
in sentences, at fourteen months, my mother
and Gwen's mother noted as they had in me
hints of melancholy, a genetic drift

my father and her father shrugged off
on their way out fishing, drunk.
They were twins, our fathers,
they were identical—our mothers, too.

Gwen's parents married in midlife,
first families wrenched apart, while Gwen
sprouted fingerbuds and toes. When she began
to speak, I made an adolescent game of asking her

what frightened her, what was a comfort,
and before long, she was asking questions back
about what made me want to know. We interviewed
each other playfully this way for years.

We looked alike; it's just, my fairness is a shade
consumptive, and the blonde a little thick with dinge,
the gray eyes slurried, gestures forced. My smile
is hesitant, my mother says suspicious. None of which,

my father thinks, is unattractive, necessarily.
But Gwen, to my mind, consummated all my shortcomings
as virtues, and with her alone I felt at ease, not
flattered, not indulged. She loved me. Me! And I,

with her, I could exist. Already you begin to see
my problem. I was bound to love her. You may think
that people choose their fate, yet how could I not
love her?—not that I ever touched her as a child.

When she began to speak, I was in high school.
Next year came the gold tips on my dogteeth.
After grad school, I was an artist, not an Artist
artist. I was what they call now a Creative.

I made ads. No one minded that you dressed in black,
or had adventures on the astral plane, and talked up
Paracelsus. All that was good packaging, for a Creative,
in L.A., only the ads I made set people's teeth on edge.

Back home, I took up teaching: art, Art
art, for ladies who disliked their husbands
(Mrs. Yearners II and III), for high school kids
who disliked high school kids (Gwen

being one of these by now). I told them,
I told her, Art celebrates what people know
and are afraid to feel. Discomfort is a measure
of its penetration. I taught them that Ugliness

could ring out the diapason of Beauty.
I did not pretend to be original, but I was
cold with passion. After a few years
at the Art Association Building

I poked up my head, out of the usual slough, and saw,
my students thought I had charisma. People wore
black jeans like mine. They smoked my brand.
They made cute, cynical remarks, and they were celibate

like me, they said. I never said that I was celibate.
They fasted, and I said I liked to eat.
Gwen, meanwhile, had been fucking everybody
nearabout lukewarm but me, and with my blessing.

This was before the epidemic. It's like
dreaming, fucking. It's impossible to talk about,
unless you lie. Friends with good friends, even,
cling to the most painfully absurd illusions.

As for family, mine forget about, and hers
broke up. They moved her into the town hotel,
into a furnished room. This was a place
where widows came to get unhappier and die.

A crack a foot wide at the mouth had opened
through the top three floors, a chasm
on a slow jag downward, like dark lightning
in a brick sky. Gwen's bedroom was under the tip.

Across the street dead level with her window,
at the steepletop, there was a bronze sculpture
of a hand fourteen feet tall, pointing skyward
to the Source of Love, and fire and brimstone.

Floyd, the desk clerk, was supposedly in loco
Gwen's parentis, but he didn't mind me
visiting, since I was practically her twin,
so long as I brought him a quart of beer.

Gwen and I brewed ginseng. We made stir fry.
You could smell her hotplate sometimes
overheating wires inside the wall. Fucking,
she said, was ridiculous. She did it

not for pleasure so much, not for power,
though she did feel pleasure, quite a bit,
and power nearly all the time. She did it
for obliteration: not to be Gwen. Gwen,

the name, she looked it up, meant White.
And she, my cousin, would be fucked
if she would be Snow White. My wheezing,
Camel-lunger's laugh would trip her sometimes

in mid-diatribe, and she laughed back
at me, and at herself. But it was irresistible,
her spiel, and I kept basking in it,
proud she spoke this way to no one else.

Their Gwen, she said, did not suggest swapfucking
doubledates. She did. And when she did
she licked the face off everybody else's marzipan.
She spirited off boy by boy, tumescent,

fretful, opening his dry lips with a moan,
and it was sweet, the way boys tried to thrill their
Gwen with clumsy self-absorption. The performances
on both sides, she said, really, could be almost

tender. Here, she caught me savoring a nuance,
and she laughed. She turned to stir
the dirty rice, and I was laughing with her,
at her, at myself, when she turned back and said,

I'll show you. She was asking, could we risk
our friendship. She intended to console me,
which I did not want. Yet she too clearly
stood in need of consolation, which aroused me,

so that I felt ashamed. She looked down, between
finding an answer in my face and answering no
herself by turning away. A globulus of dirty rice,
dislodging, tumbled from her spatula and shattered

on the carpet. We glanced up by reflex
into each other's eyes to see what we would do.
Without the rice this look would not have happened.
Fate may not be what it was. But we were on the bed

already. Later, I sat naked, smoking, staring
through the Dog Day heat outside. Gwen
lay naked on the bed. It hurt to look at her,
she looked so frail. The finger on the steeple

pointed through an empty sky toward someone
indispensable that nobody could see. Maybe
we have a chance, Gwen said. I laid my palm low
on her belly, on the most translucent skin

with those few dark hairs of adolescence
in the Sanskrit poetry of love called *romavali*.
I looked into her warm gray eyes with candor,
smiling my suspect smile, and I said, Gwen,

you tell me. Tell me how it is. And lay beside her,
touching, talking, that day, that night, and the next.
Gwen, between times, called it incest. I said we were only
cousins. Double-first cousins from two sets of twins,

Gwen argued, were genetically equivalent to siblings.
But the law found no incest; the only legal snag,
I said, was, I had raped a seventeen-year-old child,
for which the state provided I be put to death.

Gwen said that was silly; she was serious,
about the incest. I thought incest might not
be so bad. We loved each other, did we not?
And if, in the inmost stirring of her tenderness,

there was a rustle of her brother's pulse,
then good. My hidden reservation was,
I felt left out. I loved Gwen, more than I loved
anybody, ever, but without a glimmering of incest.

For her sake, I thought, I could fake the incest.
Fucking that way, God knows, the release, return
of tension, re-release, I never could have faked.
It was beyond my power to imagine. Then,

the abscess formed. I went to Dr. Yearner,
knowing I would need a root canal. X-rays
showed I needed seven root canals. To have him
do repairs, when his botchwork had caused

the damage, made no sense. I stepped in
after eighteen years grown up, and I felt
childish, trapped, and hurt. I wanted,
I don't know why I should, to please him.

There was Tweeg eating a fat nightcrawler.
Dr. Yearner rested his tremulous hands
against the bluelit glass, smiling at Tweeg
and, with a wink, at me. The Doctor's carport

was an outpost of eternity. Death's inroads
through my teeth into my head would be
transmuted here, painstakingly, into gold
under the arcane aegis of the salamander.

Gwen, meanwhile, turned down money
from the Ivy League in favor of a roofing job
in town. She got strong and tan. We both
gained weight. In her hotel room,

we were embarked. It was the night
sea journey, low wind muttering
in the shrouds, cast off in the long
boat of each other's flesh. Storms

flashed over the bronze hand. Dark
flashed back more slowly, held, and Gwen
rocked into me with, Who! and Whuh! And Ggwen!
I said. It sounded like, Go in. I clinched myself

against her, conjuring us out, not in, but out
from somewhere, out from under the cracking brick,
the muscle working, voices calling further
into the longer nights, farther and farther out.

Dr. Yearner used no anesthetic, reasoning
the nerves were dead. He drilled. I felt it.
He spoke words of comfort. And I twitched,
while Tweeg, writhing in his coffin,

pressed four-fingered hands against the glass
and stared out into the room as if he knew me
for the one who took him from his native stream
and left him here. The Doctor called me Son.

He had been drinking neat gin at the office
for ten years when I was born, in my time
slapping himself awake from Miltowns
with injected splashes of amphetamine.

And yet I watched him, as I thought Tweeg watched
from underwater, wistfully, until the burr,
vibrating, concentrated me in one spot, smoking
at the tip. Pain overflowed mere consciousness

into the cosmos. God said, quietly, Carl, you can forget
the rest. I screamed and twisted, bit the Doctor's hand,
clutching his clothes, and begging. At the end,
he slipped into the hollow of the tooth bamboo shoots

marinated in sweet essence of eucalyptus. Throbbing,
I walked out. That night, in the hotel room,
after I painted a five-rayed star in Persian blue
around Gwen's nipple so that the blood packed into it,

after I drew a circle on the tip,
smudged it with my tongue, and fell asleep,
the Doctor was in bed between us, leg on my leg,
jittery left hand tightening in my crotch.

I woke from this to stand at the window, naked,
over the blacked-out houses, smoking, looking across
at the steeple, letting the dream hand pull
again, and pull, cock stiffening. Gwen woke.

She took me back to bed, massaged my neck, said
sweet dreams, and I felt a tenderness toward her
asleep, I wished I could have felt when we made love.
Making love was what we called it now, not fucking.

Gwen's birthday that December ended my life
of statutory rape, and the statute of limitation
began to run, with Gwen pregnant, acting upbeat
for the Justice of the Peace. Floyd witnessed.

At my next appointment I found Dr. Yearner, in the chair,
not breathing. He was very light, my weight. I laid him out
on the floor, tilted his head back, lowered his jaw,
and fumbled around his tongue to clear his windpipe.

At the corner of his mouth a drop of cool spit
smeared in the stubble against my upper lip.
I could taste gin. Breathing into him did
nothing, so I set the heel of my hand

to his sternum, jabbing my full weight
into his heart five times, pause, over
and over. I could hear bones crack,
I could feel ribs coming apart when I bore down.

This whole time, I was wanting to stop, to wash
and disinfect my mouth, which now that the EMTs
had carted him away, I did. A note scotchtaped
to the aquarium said, "Sorry about this, Carl.

The overdose. Your teeth. I left you everything.
The two of you. Be loving. Have some kids.
They get money too. For all the good it did me,
I was rich. One thing, I kept hurting you on purpose.

I don't understand myself. A boy like you.
You're a good boy, Son. You'll forgive me
more than I deserve." He signed this Dr. Y.
The children, Gwen's and mine (he had none),

will inherit everything at thirty,
unless Gwen and I should split,
in which event the trust endows amphibia
at the Munich Zoo. His wives, meanwhile,

collect disbursements. Now, the carport
has become my studio. Mornings in the chair,
bemused, my drawing board across my lap, I write.
I dedicate this poem to my benefactor.

Gwen is somewhere in the house with Carl,
Carlissimo, my boy Carlino, whom I love
too much for anybody's good. The more she drinks,
the more Gwen grows deliberate. She steers

between the washer and the basement steps.
She spends the night with friends, Carl stays with me,
and mornings, in the blue light, Tweeg is writhing in here
in his coffin, pressing his pale hands against the glass.

DARK ENOUGH
TO SEE

Anonymous

Shaken by chills, I made this ink
in the usual way. I roasted copper
for the blue salts mixed with nutgall
into the river water. Feverish,
I dipped the nib of a reed
into the black pool, and before I died,
I left these curving strokes
of charactery on vellum.
I had slaughtered me a lamb.
After she turned to speak in pain,
I, who listened, flayed her
and scraped clean her skin
with that same knife I used
to cut and shape the reed, to gouge
the gall out of the living oak. This
is the skin on which I wrote. Thanks
to the deep mud where the reed grew,
thanks to the fire and water,
I made you this poem. Time
has given way. The worm
of the gallfly also died to make
this water dark enough to see.
On the bank fire speaks. Wind
and water in the same tongue
seek among the blades and stems
of the green reeds bending
under the oak limbs. God says
to the free mind, Find me.

Author's Bio

Son of a Maori priestess and a Tasmanian pirate,
Brooks Haxton at two was thrown as a human sacrifice
from the gunwale of a careening brig into a typhoon.
Becalmed for forty days, the ship, with all his kin
on board, burst into sudden flame when struck
by an exploding meteorite. The poet, raised
by porpoises and marsupial wolves, grew to serve
as a young man at Gallipoli, where in a detachment
taking ninety percent casualties he discovered the sestina
with its repeated end-words was especially suited
to his small vocabulary. For his *Sestinas Under Fire*
Haxton was awarded the Prix de Rome, the Croix de Guerre,
and Nobel Prizes in Literature, Physics, Medicine,
and several of the lesser categories. After brief stints
dancing for Diaghilev in Paris and acting under Stanislavski
in Moscow, he was sought out as a blues musician
by Charley Patton. Sick with fame and riches, he chose
anonymity as author of many of the great blues lyrics.
He was last seen over the Yazoo River east of Itta Bena,
borne in a silken hammock aloft by thousands
of ivory-billed woodpeckers. His poems now surface
through the mail with indecipherable postmarks,
in their folds fresh moultings of young ivory bills,
saffron dust, and legs of golden grasshoppers and bees.

An Early Sense of the Requirements

The one boy shrimpier than I was
started dating: Dot, a gentle girl, built
like Broderick Crawford. Teasing them made me
feel smaller, and I made it worse by reading
hedonistic prophets of abandon (Whitman, Lawrence).
I would read, and touch my prepubescence, in a mood
of wistful loathing. Teenagers like me told
girls that we read Jean-Paul Sartre, which I did.
Then, unpersuaded of results, I blundered
through Camus and over Kierkegaard, on
into Nietzsche. Now, having read books none
of the boys with pubic hair had read, I sensed
that Sartre and Camus were also pussyhounds
extraordinaires, and I would be like them,
in anguish, fierce with authenticity, but taller.

All the Immortals Ever Think About Is Sex

Nox est perpetua una dormienda   —Catullus

I'm picturing a whitewashed house, the bedroom
overlooking an olive grove by the sea.
There's wine; there's poetry; there's you, me, eros:
so: what if all this were to end at midnight?
Night, Catullus said, is sleep perpetual.
His fear of death, he thought, would put his mistress
in the mood. But soon she left him, and he died.
When I was small, I dreaded ignorance. Now,
though, all I ask is to be made forgetful
in your arms. When Heraclitus said gods know
all things are good and just, he might have meant by
"gods" eternal knowers of things truly known:
the Good, the Just, the soul's delight enacted
by the flesh. Those waking need not act and speak
as if they were asleep, he said. Though sleepy,
you and I need not be sunk in isolate
stupefaction, but may touch, while in the bay
a little square sail stiffens, and we watch, oars,
though massive to the arms of oarsmen, tiny
from our bed. And look! That tiny man on deck,
who paces and shouts orders to the crew, from here
cannot be heard under the soft crush of the waves
borne up invisibly between the sash and sill.

Clearing After Dark

Between the black rift
where the moon hung
and the grasses drenched
after a noonday downpour
the old fury in my brain
had floated far off
into the deepening calm,
as if the moon could see me
for the ghost I am.

November Seasonal

Crocuses in April broke
their muddy scab of ice,
three drops, three red drops,
swollen each as if to open
into a garnet cup, each
opening to be torn
by sleet that day.

The days grown long
grew short. Red
leaves, and everything
they fell among, fell, too.
A dark and an indifferent
cold came making themself
a place with room for us.

Seasonal

Over the rose bush smeared with yellow,
Over the maples green and red
With tar spot, like Kaposi's, on each leaf,
The Scorpion writhes on the back of the local star.
They tangle in each other's claws. The one
Chews off the other's head
By dark, and in the rain the children
Decked out as the dead come
Beg for sweets.

Lethe

Whiskey clears my thoughts.
It calms the tremor in my hand.
I lay my body on the couch
and by the lamp of alcohol read
nearly fast as I forget.

Dream Half Waking

I needed in my dream
to make a sheet of glass
into a mirror tall as me.
On my knees I worked
smoothing edges of bright foil
as if I thought the sun
were leakage I could stop.

On Re-Reading Hillman in the
Light of Heraclitus

"...all icons gone, the soul begins again..."

My wife and children while I'm reading sleep.
The paperback from twenty years ago
keeps crumbling, pages yellowed where the air
and acids in the fiber cook. The glue
exposed along the shattered binding turns
to powder on my fingertips. It smells
like smoke I breathed when I took out the trash
and burned it as a boy. But look what's happened
to the boy's hand, how the veins bulge, and the spotted
wrinkles purse around them, withered in the same
slow oven as the book. Anyone, the author says,
embarked upon a program of transcendence
has been duped by wistfulness rigidified
in dogma. Of their own weight pages loosen,
falling to my lap and to the floor. Snowflakes
at the lower margins of the panes drift,
in the night beyond, a few blurred spots
of light. The calm inside the quiet falls
away. In sleep, my twin girls, both of them
at once, shift poses, though as six-year-olds
less often than they did at two, still sometimes:
swimmers now, now dancers, divers in free-fall.
Their older brother's face is mine at his age,
watchful in a dream, the way I was when flames
rose out of the papers in the trash, hypnotic,
white space from around the words drawn off,
what had been local news a curl of ash now
torn, pulled into the updraft through the fire.
It glows again, that tissue in the flame.
It glows, and falls still glowing in the grass.

Ink

Somewhere God knows in the Bronx
past midnight I was speeding
past big auto shops warehouses lots
my drunk friend nervous asking me
if I knew where we were And me
with tears about to come from laughing
never having been so lost

My friend kept disappearing in the speed
The laughter disconnecting us The tears
And no one on the street The children
that next morning wrote me poems
Eight-year-olds collected
from the playground fence crack vials
their teacher ought to see

One girl raised her hand She said
her *Ahn-tee* died that week of AIDS
Her blank face and her friends'
were clues My feelings felt
beside the point The point was hidden
Everything kept spinning Late news
Sleep And in the morning paper ink

It Comes to Me: Concision!

One two three: up: and between
the ramp and the bed of the truck,
as we shifted grips, my filing cabinet
separated just enough from the dolly, in air,
for me to slip my right thumb into the gap.

When it hit, I felt: *grandes oeuvres:* play, lay,
epic, sequences epistolary, meditative, meta-narrative,
and essayistic, essay, film script, everything,
crank correspondence, refutations of rejection,
every word I wrote and kept, I felt smack on my thumb.

My thumbnail has retained for months the shape
of crimped and beaten-open pipe. François Villon
said in his shortest and to me most memorable
poem that from a fathom of rope his neck
would learn the weight of his ass.

Instructions for the Dead

When you find the River Fire,
follow it where sulfur
hotsprings under a queasy steam
decline at nightfall
into the lowland of black poplars.

Skeletons of ancient willows
litter the dirt with limbs.
Fire spills into a second river,
Lamentation. Ripplings shush
past canyon walls so close

the only path now takes you
thigh deep into the warm grip,
into the sting and wrench of water
under an arch where the cave
in the pure dark narrowing

turns down. Stoop. Lay your face
on the water plunging
airless into the rock.
Let the bitterness fill
your nostrils. Let the heaviness

soothe your lungs. Nothing
is left in you to drown.
Let the current bear you
into the underchannel. There
the River Lamentation empties

into the subterranean River Sadness.
Do not search for the ferryman
or the ferry. Let the obol
fall from your mouth.
No one here receives payment.

No one sees the bronze coin
flutter onto the black floor
deep in coins with images
of owls of wisdom skimmed
by the now insensate fingers.

Sadness empties into the great
cave of the River Anger.
Overhead brown air, in silence
corpses face down
on the infinite dead water.

Time has ended, but not Anger.
Souls at the far shore
walk adazzle
into the fields
of nameless flowers

thirsty for the springs
of the Forgotten.
But the mind too hurt
to unconfuse floats face down
in the Slough of Anger.

Sanskrit by First Snowfall

Under the dust a flake of consciousness,
a word, a condensation frozen on the breath,
is falling fallen windblown whirling:
Krishna on the white flake of the lotus
in the arms of Lakshmi, hands divine
inside each other's shirt. And all around them
wheels of heaven crash into the silent
windows of Bird Library past midnight,
Bird of the Dead Tongues, mine, my logy
snowbird Ba in snow. I should be home.
My daughters my twin girls say Ba for bird
for book for bottle—Ba: in Egypt,
bird with a human head, the soul.
They wake and wake their mother. Ba!
They point into the dark. Ba, Ba! they say,
and back to nursing weary in her arms.

A Note About the Author

Brooks Haxton, born in Greenville, Mississippi, in 1950, is the son of the novelist Ellen Douglas and the composer Kenneth Haxton. He has published two book-length narrative poems and three previous collections of poetry, most recently *The Sun at Night* (1995). His book of translations of ancient Greek poetry, *Dances for Flute and Thunder,* was one of three nominees for the 2000 PEN Poetry in Translation Award. He wrote the script for *Tennessee Williams: Orpheus of the American Stage,* a film broadcast in the American Masters Series on PBS in 1995, and has been the recipient of fellowships from the National Endowment for the Arts, the National Endowment for the Humanities, and the John Simon Guggenheim Foundation, among other institutions. He is currently the director of the Syracuse University M.F.A. Program in Creative Writing.

A Note on the Type

The text of this book was set in a typeface called Aldus, designed by the celebrated typographer Hermann Zapf in 1952–1953. Based on the classical proportion of the popular Palatino type family, Aldus was originally adapted for Linotype composition as a slightly lighter version that would read better in smaller sizes.

Hermann Zapf was born in Nuremberg, Germany, in 1918. He has created many other well-known typefaces, including Comenius, Hunt Roman, Marconi, Melior, Michelangelo, Optima, Saphir, Sistina, Zapf Book and Zapf Chancery.

Composed by Creative Graphics,
Allentown, Pennsylvania
Printed and bound by Edwards Brothers,
Ann Arbor, Michigan
Designed by Anthea Lingeman